our songs, our places, without you

our songs, our places, without you

trevor capiro

Dedicated to everyone who has ever wished they could take back the love they gave to someone who didn't deserve it.

our songs, our places, without you

CHAPTERS

our songs, our places, without you

<u>*Chapter One*</u>

trevor capiro

our songs

you said
it was our song

perfect

just like us

i was a fool
for ever believing you

i used to look at you
and feel
a deep longing

now i look at photos of us
and wonder how
i was so blind
that i couldn't see
what was right in front of me...

i wish i could travel
back in time
and tell
the younger version of myself
not to worry, think, and cry
far too much
about you

the pain
was never
worth it

don't fuck with my love.

i will give you
everything i have
but if you hurt me
i will never

-

f o r g e t

i gave you
love
affection
sex
& energy

you gave me
pain
heartbreak
tears
& trust issues.

i wish
i could tell my heart
what my brain has known
for so long

you
are nothing but pain
to me

your compliments
were like candy

temporarily sweet
to the tongue
but bitter
to the heart
in the long run

maybe i deserved
all of the heartbreak
you caused me;

after all,
i was foolish enough
to give my heart
to someone
so cruel.

in the end
nothing on this planet
matters
more than the simple
human moments
in day to day life

i am still here
still standing
despite
~~*your best*~~
efforts

do you really
want to date him

or are you just
lonely?

tear down the walls between us.

let's make it right
and try
to start again.

if i could get on a plane
tomorrow
and start a whole new life
with no trace
of your memory
believe me, i would

all the songs
we sang together
all the lyrics
that meant so much
to us

you threw it all away
and now these songs
i once loved
are poison to my ears

do not accept
anything less
than all the love
you deserve

if you're just in it when its easy
you're not really in it
at all.

i spent too long
thinking about
how good i would feel
if you finally
came to your senses
and begged to have me back

now i realize
i wasted too many good moments
thinking about you
when you

if they don't care enough
to text you back
and reassure you
that they care

they're just not worth it.

i fell too fast

*you laughed
as i drowned*

you never cared about me
you only cared
about what you could get from me.

i wish
i could forget you

but instead
the thoughts of you
are burning
like an eternal flame
in my mind

nothing reveals
a man's weakness
like the way
he is threatened
by a woman
who is not entranced
by his bullshit

if only your actions
loved me
the way
your words did

we could still be
happy
right now ...

but what if your
actions <u>hurt</u> the way your
words did?

trevor capiro

our songs, our places, without you

Chapter Two

trevor capiro

our places

i hate this town
but more than that
i hate the way
i used to love it
until
you ruined it for me

now i cannot even walk
down my home street
without running in
to memories of you

all you can do
is live your life
day by day
not worrying
too much
about tomorrow

do not waste your time
on someone
who swears they will change
but never does

their lies
will only get worse
as time goes on

last night i saw you
sitting in the cafe
by the window
with someone else
already moved on
replacing me
in the exact spot
we used to sit

it pains me to see
how easy it was
for you to move on

make this the year
of cutting toxic people
out of your life

*you were never in love with me
you were just lonely.*

you cannot chase after
someone else
without losing
pieces
of yourself
along the way

i wish i saw your selfishness
for what it was
instead of mistaking it
for love

do not be afraid
to be
a work in progress

starry night
was not painted in an instant
and your perfect life
will take time, too.

every tear
you made me cry
every kiss
i wasted on you

each one was a lesson
that i will never forget.

you are enough
you are enough
you are enough
you are enough
you are enough

never stop believing this
plant it so deeply
in your mind
that no one
can take it away rom you

memories of your touch
haunt my skin
the hairs on my arms
stand up
in the exact places
your fingers
used to rest

illusion

i thought
we were in this
together

apparently
it was just me
carrying the weight
of both of us
on my shoulders

some apologies
cannot be accepted

sometimes the pain
is too powerful
to be painted over
so easily

why does everyone
have to leave?

i wish i could feel
anything
as deeply
as i feel
the heartbreak
of losing you

*as i let you go
i knew i was letting go
of the best
and worst
thing
i've ever had.*

i fell in love
with you

but it turns out
that was just
a version of you
you made for me
to get what you wanted

i get attached too easily
i love too hard, too fast

but i can't believe
i was dumb enough to believe you
when you said
"i love you".

you cannot truly heal
while you are looking to others
for healing

true healing
must come from within

i used to think
i would never feel complete
without you

now i wonder
how i ever let you
keep me down
for so long

isolation

my insecurities
believed you
when you screamed at me
that i would always need you

your love
was poisoned chocolate

tasting so sweet
but hurting so terribly.

i will never get an explanation
from you
for why i wasn't good enough
and it's time
i accepted that

do not waste
your rays of sunshine
on seeds
which will never bloom

if he lets you
go to bed
upset

he doesn't care
about you

our songs, our places, without you

*i wish i wasn't so good
at ruining
good things*

trevor capiro

our songs, our places, without you

Chapter Three

without you

all those sad songs
i used to skip
suddenly
mean the world to me
when i think of you

a life without risk
is not a life at all

freedom, to me
means finally
letting go
of you.

& the anger
you gave me

i hope that time
shows you
how much you lost
when you let go
of me

you were a drug
my veins craved more
of you
even though my mind knew
you did nothing but hurt me

you cannot heal
a broken bone
if you never get up
from where you fell

[you cannot heal
a broken heart
if you never leave
the one who hurt you]

i should have paid
more attention
to all the little clues
you showed

i wish i could take
a handful of balloons
and float away
to another place
and start
a new life

i want to leave you
but i know
before long
i would find myself
sending you texts
in moments of weakness
reopening wounds
that had only just begun
to heal

if you're wondering
if it's time to move on

it is.

i can't say that i regret
our time together
for although it hurt
more than anything
it also taught me
more lessons
than anything else.

never beg someone
to be part of your life.

if you have to beg them,
they don't deserve
your time, love, or energy.

stop holding on
to things of the past

there is no use
in re-opening old wounds
that could've healed long ago
if you left them alone

i traced a finger
along your freckles
as if i was tracing constellations
in the stars

it hurts to lose
your greatest comfort

your arms were a home to me
and now i wander the streets
aimless and hurt

if you love someone
just tell them

life is short
there's no use
in missing out
on living it to the fullest.

there is no greater feeling
than knowing
that you're doing just fine
without someone
who you used to need.

your time is too valuable
to waste
on people
who can't make up their mind
if they want you or not

our songs, our places, without you

it's okay to protect your heart
and refuse to take chances on people
who are just going to let you down

i am tired of holding back what i really want to say. i am tired of pushing my tongue down instead of speaking my mind. from now on i will never silence myself again. i will never change myself for others. i will never compromise my own happiness for someone else.

to my future self, this i promise you: i will give you the freedom you always dreamed of.

do me a favor
and leave me alone
if you're only planning
on using me
and breaking my heart.

the greatest struggle
of getting over someone
is staying strong
keeping your mind off of them
and suddenly
out of the blue
something reminds you of them
and suddenly
you're hurting
all over again

sadness hurts
but it is necessary

just as a wound
must be cleaned
before it can heal

[so you must be sad
before your heart can heal]
and be ready
to love again

trevor capiro

our songs, our places, without you

Chapter Four

trevor capiro

healing

[*if it takes*
the rest of my life
i will slowly chip away
at your hold on my mind
until one day
i will wake up
without the curse
of thoughts of you]

and on that day
i will rejoice
knowing that i
am truly free
at last

*don't fall in love
with people
who are still in love
with someone else*

*all they're doing
is looking
for pieces of who they want
in you*

i wish i could make
that pretty perfect life
for us
in real life
as easily as i do
in every careless daydream

your smile
is the most beautiful sunrise

you are the only one
you truly need

the worst thing
you can do
for yourself
is settle
for mediocre
love, sex, wine, or life

sometimes you have to accept
that you'll never get an answer
about why it ended

though we feel we need
closure
sometimes we must accept
that we'll never get it

you need to reach a point
where you want more
than just
someone
to distract you
from the loneliness

Anxiety:

so many times
the smallest snowball
has rolled itself down
the slopes of my mind
and made a disaster
out of the smallest problem

there is nothing more powerful
than a woman
who is fully aware
of everything
she deserves

you silenced me
you took away my voice

now i have finally
freed myself

i forgot how good it feels
to speak for myself

you deserve to be loved
as if you have no past
and don't carry the weight
of past failed loves

nothing hurts quite as much
as someone telling you
they love you
and then leaving

i will
find someone
to love me
in all the ways
you never could

& there were a lot.

i was prepared for the pain
of broken bones and cut skin
but nothing could prepare me
for the pain
of losing someone
who once
meant everything to me

sometimes you just have to accept
that the one you want
just isn't the right one
for you.

you are the storm

you cannot tame your spirit
to comfort someone
too weak to handle
your passion

you promised
to meet me halfway
but i was always the one
going all the way
for you

if it's not going to matter
in 5 years
don't spend
more than 5 minutes
worrying about it

i should never have let
you
mistake
my kindness
for weakness

at last, i let you go
burning the letters
you wrote me

i am taking back
our songs
i am taking back
our places
i am taking back
myself

tonight, i'm letting you go
for good.

-*trevor capiro*

our songs, our places, without you

thank you for reading my debut collection of poetry! if you liked the book, please leave a nice review on amazon as it really helps other people find it. tell your friends and post about it on social media! with your help, anything is possible.

i hope to write you another book soon.

all my love,

-trevor capiro